breakfast in a cookie jar

quick and easy grab and go bars to make your day yummier

Elder Memmott, I hope you give some of these a try. Love, Carlene Duda

CARLENE DUDA

author of beyond oatmeal *and* completely breakfast

CFI
Springville, Utah

ISBN: 978-1-59955-337-5

Published by CFI, an imprint of Cedar Fort, Inc., 2373 W. 700 S., Springville, UT 84663
Distributed by Cedar Fort, Inc., www.cedarfort.com

LIBRARY OF CONGRESS CATALOGING-IN-PUBLICATION DATA

Duda, Carlene, 1962-
  Breakfast in a cookie jar / Carlene Duda.
    p. cm.
  ISBN 978-1-59955-337-5 (acid-free paper)
  1. Cookies 2. Breakfasts
  TX772 .D83 2009
  641.8/654 22
                    2009032487

Cover and page design by Jen Boss
Edited by Heidi Doxey
Cover design © 2009 by Lyle Mortimer

Printed in the United States of America

10 9 8 7 6 5 4 3 2 1

Printed on acid-free paper

contents

"Life is too short—stay awake for it."

introduction

It all started with an Easy-Bake Oven. That's right—I have one of the original 1963, turquoise-green Easy-Bake Ovens complete with baking set and recipe cookbook.

My twin sister, Connie, and I would plug in the oven and watch that 100-watt lightbulb perform its magic. I really thought that the temperature knobs on the front actually controlled the heat. One batch of cookie dough or a cake mix and you could be baking to your hearts' content.

My children have all followed in the same tradition of Easy-Bake Oven cookie-baking. It's ironic that my children watch DVDs, play CDs, listen to iPods, and discuss megapixels and gigabytes, and yet they were quite awestruck when they realized they were really, in fact, baking with only a single lightbulb.

I didn't grow up in a household where we baked a lot of cookies. Cakes were the dessert of choice. My mom claimed it was a time issue. With a cake, you mix it up, pour the batter into the pan, throw the pan into the oven and *voilà*—375 degrees and 35 minutes later—you've got dessert.

Growing up in Washington State meant we had a large Gravenstein apple tree in our backyard. When the apples were in season, my dad would announce to my sister and me that we would be taking turns every Saturday and making two apple pies. This involved going outside and choosing the right apples under the tree; peeling; coring; slicing; cutting in the shortening; always rolling the dough too thin; playing with the dough, thus causing it to become dry and tough; and finally piecing the top crust together, making it appear like a patchwork quilt. Of course, being teenagers, we managed to prolong the pie-making process into an agonizing all-day experience.

It wasn't until my college years that I truly understood and appreciated my pie-making training. I quickly learned that a girl who could bake a great pie had an advantage when it came to hungry college guys, and I could bake a great pie! Need I say more?

After college, I discovered that cakes and pies were simply not enough when it came to baking for a husband and children. Cookies are almost a prerequisite when raising four children. Sadly, my cookie-baking experience and skill level was limited to my Easy-Bake Oven days. It was time to graduate from my single-bulb oven to a full-grown convection oven. The pressure was on, and I was definitely in trouble.

Anytime I attended an event where there were home-baked cookies, I was on the prowl. I was not above stalking and pursuing a pastry-cook until I could get the recipe—family secret or not. My motives were justified by my inability to bake a decent cookie. My family was always willing to support and validate the purpose of my mission. My persistent begging caused my collection of cookie recipes to flourish. Since I had no lack of taste-testing volunteers, with perseverance and plenty of practice, I am pleased to say I have become an excellent and accomplished cookie and cookie bar baker.

Breakfast *In a Cookie Jar* is the third in my series of breakfast cookbooks. *Beyond Oatmeal: 101 Breakfast Recipes* focuses on wonderful breads, pancakes, waffles, French toast, crumb cakes, and more. *Completely Breakfast* complements *Beyond Oatmeal* with hearty potato casseroles, omelets, eggs, breakfast sandwiches, and smoothies. *Breakfast in a Cookie Jar* offers recipes for easy-to-make cookies and bars for those who would like an alternative to traditional breakfast foods. These cookies and bars can also be used for everything from cold cereals to grab and go snacks. They make great healthy desserts for lunches, after school snacks, and treats for any time.

the morning meal

Rise, Shine, and Dine

One of the most common nutritional mistakes many people make is skipping the morning meal. There are plenty of reasons why people do this: some are too busy to prepare something; others think that saving the calories from this meal will help them with weight loss; and others simply don't like breakfast foods.

To make sure your family members get the nutrition they need, make breakfast a family meal whenever you can. Shared meals provide valuable opportunities for families to reconnect.

Remember, the morning meal doesn't have to be all about traditional breakfast items. Making breakfast a self-serve meal for kids and the family can help relieve some of the anxiety during the morning rush. These cookies and bars will make it convenient for you to use a grab-and-go approach—whether it is for a breakfast on the run or an afternoon snack. Planning ahead and keeping it simple is a great way to start your day.

Skipping breakfast can mean going as long as fourteen hours without refueling your tank. That's too long for anyone who wants to succeed. You wouldn't try to drive to school or work on an empty gas tank and you shouldn't allow your body or mind to go on an empty tank, either.

cookie tips

- Read each recipe carefully before starting. Be sure you have all the ingredients called for and that you understand the recipe clearly.
- Preheat the oven before you begin baking your cookies. This is usually a good practice, although there are some recipes that specifically call for you to start with a cold oven.
- Accurately measure your ingredients with standard measuring cups and spoons.
- Take care not to overmix your dough or beat it too vigorously after adding the flour—if you do, your cookies will be tough.
- To get cookies with uniform thickness and size, use cookie or ice cream scoops. Having your cookies the same size guarantees they will bake in the same amount of time.
- A good rule of thumb is to leave 2 inches between each cookie-dough ball when placing them on the baking sheet.
- Use shiny aluminum pans for baking cookies, so the cookies will brown evenly and lightly. Dark sheets tend to absorb the heat and will overbrown the bottoms of your cookies. If you use insulated baking sheets, remember that since the bottom does not brown as fast as with regular pans, you may need a longer baking time.
- You can use margarine or butter interchangeably unless a recipe specifically calls for one or the other. Butter and margarine give cookies their flavor and crisp outside texture. When a recipe calls for solid shortening, it will usually produce a cookie with a crunchy texture. Shortening can usually be substituted for margarine or butter; however, remember that 1 cup butter equals 1 cup plus 2 tablespoons shortening. Using whipped butter or low-calorie butter

can often ruin the recipe. Whipped or low-calorie spreads have added air and water in them and will change the consistency of the recipe. Most cookies call for softened butter for the best blending consistency. To soften your butter, let it stand at room temperature for 30 to 45 minutes. Be careful not to let it soften too long as this can result in dough that is too soft.

- Don't grease pans with butter or margarine; use solid shortening. Butter tends to make cookies brown too fast, and oils and sprays tend to cause sticking.
- Cool cookies on wire racks. This will allow the steam to evaporate and will keep your cookies from becoming soggy.
- Use a pancake turner to remove your cookies from the baking sheets. This will keep warm cookies from tearing or breaking.
- Watch the baking time. Always check cookies at the minimum baking time. Even one minute can mean the difference between a cookie that is done and one that is ruined. Immediately remove cookies from the baking sheet, unless the recipe calls for the cookies to cool for a specified time on the cookie sheet.

bar cookie tips

Have you ever wondered why bars and squares are categorized as cookies and not as cakes? It is because bar cookies and squares have a batter that is dense and has a cookielike texture. Bar cookies and squares are casual desserts, for, unlike cookies, which require the batter to be is dropped in mounds, formed into balls, or cut into shapes and placed on a baking sheet, the batter is simply spread into a pan. It is only after baking that bar cookies or squares are cut into individual portions.

- Brownies and cakelike bars are usually done when they pull away from the sides of the pan, when a toothpick inserted in the center of the brownies comes out clean, or when the center is set. However, its harder to determine when some bars and brownies are done. Use the specified time listed on the recipe. Just remember that overbaking will produce dry and brittle brownies and bars.
- Make sure that you use the appropriate size pan as determined by the recipe. A pan that is too big can cause dry bars, while one that is too small can cause underbaked bars.
- Lining pans with foil makes it easier to remove your bars.
- Make sure to allow bars to cool before trying to cut them, unless the recipe says to cut them while hot. Otherwise, you'll just end up with a crumbled mess.

storing

You should always allow all cookies and bar cookies to cool completely before trying to store them.

- Soft Cookies should be placed between sheets of waxed paper in an airtight container. Make sure the container has a snug-fitting lid. If the cookies begin to dry out, put a slice of bread on a sheet of waxed paper and place inside the container. Replace the slice of bread as needed.
- Crispy Cookies should be stored in a container with a loose-fitting lid unless you live in a humid climate. If the humidity is high where you live, store these cookies in an airtight container as well.
- Frosted Cookies should be stored only after the frosting has set on the cookies. Like soft cookies, all frosted cookies should be stored between layers of waxed paper. It is best if you do not stack the layers deeper than three layers.

freezing

Most cookie dough will freeze exceptionally well and can be kept frozen for up to three months. Just let the dough defrost in the refrigerator, but plan ahead as this will take several hours.

- Freeze cookies only after they are completely cooled.
- To freeze unfrosted cookies, layer them in a freezer-safe container or resealable plastic freezer bag. Use a sheet of waxed paper between each layer.
- To freeze frosted cookies, arrange cookies on a tray in a single layer and freeze until firm. Then place the frozen cookies in a freezer-safe plastic bag.

Make sure to label cookies with the date that you froze them clearly marked. Cookies should keep up to six months in a proper storage container. To thaw, remove from container and loosely cover. Allow cookies to stand at room temperature for 10–20 minutes.

fruits & nuts

Almond Cranberry Granola Bars

Fantastic bars that have a lot of flexibility. Great for hikes, long road trips, and camping! Use any combination of chocolate chips, dried fruit, coconut, pecans, almond slices, or any other tidbits you'd like in a granola bar!

3 cups oats

1 (14-oz.) can sweetened condensed milk

2 Tbsp. butter, melted

1 cup sliced almonds

½ cup cranberries, dried

1 cup flaked coconut

1 cup miniature semisweet chocolate chips

Preheat oven to 350 degrees. Grease a 13x9-inch pan.

In a large bowl, mix together the oats, milk, butter, almonds, cranberries, coconut, and chocolate chips. Mix with your hands until well blended.

Press flat into the prepared pan.

Bake for 20–25 minutes until lightly browned just around the edges. This will give you chewy bars.

Let cool for 5 minutes. Cut into squares and then let cool completely before serving.

Makes 24 bars.

Apple Breakfast Bars

A nutritious way to help satisfy hunger with great tasting fruit, nuts and grains!

In a large bowl, combine all ingredients together. Let stand 10 minutes. Press mixture into an 8x8-inch baking pan.

Bake at 375 degrees until lightly browned, about 25 minutes. Loosen with a spatula and cut into bars while warm.

Makes 16 2x2-inch bars.

1½ cups quick-rolled oats

¼ cup whole wheat flour

⅔ cup dates, chopped

½ cup walnuts, chopped

½ tsp. salt

¼ cup orange juice

1½ cups apple (peeled, cored, and shredded)

Banana Granola Cookies

½ cup margarine, softened

1 cup brown sugar, firmly packed

1 egg

1 tsp. vanilla

1 cup banana, mashed

1½ cups flour

1 tsp. cinnamon

1½ tsp. baking soda

1½ tsp. salt

1 cup granola

Preheat oven to 375 degrees.

Grease 2 cookie sheets.

In a large bowl, cream the margarine and brown sugar. Add the egg, vanilla, and banana, beating until well blended. Add the flour, cinnamon, baking soda, and salt and mix until blended. Stir in the granola.

Drop by the tablespoon onto the prepared cookie sheet, spacing about 2 inches apart.

Bake for 12 minutes. Cool on a wire rack.

Makes 4 dozen.

Banana-Oatmeal Breakfast Bars

At your desk or on the road, these handy oat bars fit conveniently into a purse, briefcase, workout bag, backpack, or lunch box. Wholesome goodness and the great taste of bananas and walnuts!

Preheat oven to 425 degrees.

Grease and flour 13x9-inch baking pan.

Sift together flour, salt, cinnamon, nutmeg, and baking soda. Set aside.

In a large bowl, beat butter, brown sugar, and egg until light and fluffy.

Add bananas and vanilla, beating until smooth. Gradually stir in flour mixture and oats until well combined. (If it seems to be getting a little thick, slowly add a few tablespoons of milk as needed.) Stir in raisins and nuts.

Bake for 25 minutes until golden brown. Cut into bars.

1½ cups flour
1 tsp. salt
1 tsp. cinnamon
½ tsp. nutmeg
½ tsp. baking soda
½ cup butter, softened
1 cup brown sugar, packed
1 egg
1 cup (3 medium) bananas, mashed
1½ tsp. vanilla
1½ cups oats
½ cup raisins
½ cup walnuts, chopped

Blueberry Breakfast Bars

Versatility should be this bar's middle name. Change the filling flavor to apple or cherry, and they will always be irresistible!

1¾ cup sugar

1 cup butter

4 eggs

2 tsp. vanilla

3 cup flour

1½ tsp. baking powder

1 (21-oz.) can blueberry pie filling

1¼ cup powdered sugar

2 Tbsp. lemon juice

1 Tbsp. margarine, melted

Preheat oven to 350 degrees.

Cream sugar and butter, add eggs and vanilla. Beat well. Add flour and baking powder. Stir until blended.

Spread half of the mixture onto an ungreased 15x10-inch jelly-roll pan. Carefully top with pie filling.

Drop remaining dough on top by teaspoonfuls. Bake for 45 minutes or until golden brown. Do not underbake.

Combine powdered sugar, lemon juice, and melted margarine and drizzle over warm bars.

Makes 25 bars.

Cranberry Oatmeal Cookies

From first sight to first bite, you'll be quite delighted!
Breakfast cookies are the wave of the future!

Preheat oven to 350 degrees.

Blend butter and sugar until fluffy. Add eggs and vanilla and mix well.

In a separate bowl, sift flours, baking soda, and salt together. Stir into butter mixture. Stir in oats. Fold in cranberries and nuts.

Drop spoonfuls of cookie dough onto ungreased cookie sheets, spaced at least 2 inches apart.

Bake 8–10 minutes. Cool on wire racks.

Makes 2 dozen.

- ½ cup plus 2 Tbsp. butter
- ⅔ cup brown sugar, packed
- 1 tsp. vanilla
- 2 eggs
- 1½ tsp. baking soda
- pinch salt
- 1¼ cup flour
- ⅔ cup whole wheat flour
- 1 cup oats
- 2 cups cranberries
- ¾ cup walnuts, chopped

Frosted Carrot Bars

You're invited to be delighted with cream cheese frosting covering this luscious moist carrot bar!

1 cup butter, softened

1 cup honey

3 eggs

1 tsp. vanilla

1½ cups flour

1½ tsp. baking soda

1 tsp. ground cinnamon

¾ tsp. salt

¾ cup walnuts, chopped

1½ cups carrots, shredded

Frosting:

1 cup powdered sugar

8 oz. cream cheese

1 tsp. vanilla

1 tsp. milk

Preheat oven to 350 degrees. Grease a 15x10-inch jelly roll pan.

In a large mixing bowl, combine butter, honey, eggs, vanilla, flour, baking soda, cinnamon, and salt. Beat for about 2 minutes at low speed, scraping bowl often, until well mixed. By hand, stir in walnuts and carrots.

Spread into prepared pan.

Bake for 20–25 minutes or until top springs back when touched lightly in center. Cool completely.

In a small mixing bowl, combine all frosting ingredients. Beat at medium speed, scraping bowl often, until smooth (about 2 minutes). Spread frosting on cooled bars, cut into bars, and store in refrigerator.

Makes 4 dozen bars.

German Chocolate Snack Bars

This bar is for the mothers only at the play date.
They are sure to impress anyone with a sweet tooth.

Preheat oven to 325 degrees. Grease a 13x9-inch baking dish.

In a medium saucepan, melt chocolate and butter over low heat. Remove pan from heat. Add ½ cup sweetened condensed milk, eggs, baking mix, and vanilla. Stir until well blended.

Spread batter evenly into prepared baking dish.

In a medium bowl, combine the remaining condensed milk with the coconut. Spoon evenly over batter in baking dish. Sprinkle nuts over the top, pressing them down firmly.

Bake for 25 minutes, or until done. Cool and cut into bars.

Makes 18 bars.

4 (1-oz.) squares German sweet chocolate

¼ cup butter

1 (14-oz.) can sweetened condensed milk, reserving ½ cup

2 eggs

½ cup baking mix

1 tsp. vanilla

1 cup flaked coconut

1 cup chopped pecans

Honey-Fruit Trail Mix Bars

Who doesn't like the chewy flavor of a tasty granola bar?
Cranberries, raisins, and almonds will give you
all the energy you need to keep on hiking!

4½ cups oats

1 cup flour

1 tsp. cinnamon

1 tsp. baking soda

1½ tsp. vanilla

⅔ cup butter, softened

½ cup brown sugar, packed

½ cup honey

½ cup miniature semisweet chocolate chips

½ cup cranberries, dried

½ cup almonds, sliced

½ cup raisins

Preheat oven to 325 degrees. Lightly grease a 13x9-inch pan.

In a large bowl, combine the first four ingredients. Add vanilla, butter, brown sugar, and honey. Beat with an electric mixer. Batter will be very heavy. Using a spoon, stir in chocolate chips, cranberries, almonds, and raisins.

Press dough into prepared pan. Bake 20–25 minutes until golden brown.

Cool in pan 10 minutes.

Cut into snack-size bars and cool completely before removing from pan.

Oat Cake Bars

Delicious bars don't necessarily require a long list of ingredients.

Preheat oven to 375 degrees. Grease a 13x9-inch pan.

Combine cake mix and oats in a large bowl; stir in the melted butter until the mixture is crumbly. Measure half of this mixture (about 3 cups) into the greased pan. Press firmly into pan to cover the bottom.

Combine the jam and water; spoon over crumb mixture in pan and spread evenly. Cover with the remaining crumb mixture. Pat firmly to make top even.

Bake for 20 minutes; top should be very light brown. Cool completely before cutting into bars.

Makes 20 bars

¾ **cup butter or margarine, melted**

1 **(18.25 oz.) package yellow cake mix**

2½ **cups oats**

1½ **cups jam, any flavor of your choice**

1 **Tbsp. water**

Raspberry Oat Bars

Tasty oat bars with a zippy layer of raspberry in the center and crunch on the top!

¾ cup butter, softened

1 cup brown sugar, packed

1½ cups oats

1½ cups flour

1 tsp. salt

½ tsp. baking powder

1¼ cups raspberry jam

powdered sugar

Preheat oven to 400 degrees.

Grease a 13x9-inch pan.

In a large bowl, cream together the butter and brown sugar until smooth.

Combine the oats, flour, salt, and baking powder; stir into the creamed mixture.

Press half of the mixture into the bottom of the prepared pan. Spread the raspberry jam over the top of the pressed mixture.

Crumble the remaining crust mixture over the raspberry layer.

Bake for 20–25 minutes until light brown. Cool completely before cutting into bars. Dust with powdered sugar.

Makes 24 bars.

Breakfast in a Cookie Jar

Robust Energy Bars

*Major ingredients, major flavor! It might look like a lot of work,
but once you have made these bars you will want to make them again.*

Place oats and sliced almonds on a baking sheet. Toast in preheated oven at 300 degrees for 10 minutes. Set aside to cool. Turn the oven to 325 degrees.

Place raisins, apricots, oats, and almonds in a food processor. Pulse about 10 times until coarsely chopped. Set aside.

In the bowl of a heavy-duty mixer fitted with a paddle, beat the butter, brown sugar, molasses, and egg until light and fluffy.

In a separate bowl, combine both flours, dry milk, wheat germ, baking soda, baking powder, vanilla, and salt. Add to the creamed mixture. Mix thoroughly. Add dried fruit mixture.

Butter a 13x9-inch baking pan. Pour in the batter and spread evenly. Bake for about 30 minutes or until set.

Cool in the pan. Cut into 4-inch bars.

To store, wrap bars individually in plastic wrap. The bars will keep for about one week. Freeze for up to three months.

- 1 cup quick-cooking oats
- ½ cup sliced almonds
- ½ cup dark raisins
- ½ cup golden raisins
- ½ cup dried apricots
- ½ cup unsalted butter, at room temperature
- ½ cup brown sugar
- ¼ cup golden molasses
- 1 egg
- 1 cup whole wheat flour
- 1 cup flour
- ½ cup nonfat dry milk
- ¼ cup toasted wheat germ
- ½ tsp. baking soda
- 1½ tsp. baking powder
- 1 tsp. vanilla
- pinch salt
- ½ cup 2 percent milk
- 1 Tbsp. unsalted butter for buttering pan

Triple Peanut Cookies

Indulge the peanut lovers in your family with three types
of peanut flavors they will never forget!

- **1¼ cups brown sugar, packed**
- **1 cup sugar**
- **1 cup butter, softened**
- **¾ cup chunky peanut butter**
- **½ tsp. salt**
- **2 eggs**
- **2 cups flour**
- **½ tsp. baking soda**
- **1 cup peanut butter chips**
- **1 cup dry roasted salted peanuts**

Preheat oven to 350 degrees.

Mix together both sugars, butter, peanut butter, and salt.

Beat eggs into mixture until light and fluffy.

In a separate bowl, sift together flour and baking soda. Gradually blend into sugar mixture. Stir in peanut butter chips and salted peanuts.

Drop by tablespoonfuls 2 inches apart on a greased baking sheet.

Bake 9–10 minutes or until lightly brown around the edges.

Makes 4 dozen cookies.

cereal

Apple Harvest Bars

This apple bar has a real crush on fruit!

1 cup plus 2 Tbsp. shortening, divided

2¾ cups flour

1 tsp. salt

milk

1 egg yolk, beaten (save egg white)

1 cup wheat flake cereal, crushed

7–8 cups apples, pared and thinly sliced

⅔ cup sugar

½ tsp. cinnamon

¼ tsp. allspice

1 cup powdered sugar

1–2 Tbsp. water

1 tsp. vanilla

¼ cup nuts, finely chopped

Preheat oven to 350 degrees. Cut shortening into flour and salt until particles are the size of small peas. Add enough milk to egg yolk to measure ⅔ cup. Stir into flour mixture until pastry almost cleans side of bowl.

Gather pastry into ball; divide into 2 equal parts. Shape each part into a flattened round on a lightly floured board. Roll 1 part into rectangle, 15x10 inches, with rolling pin; fold into thirds. Place in jelly roll pan, unfold to cover bottom of pan. Sprinkle crushed cereal on pastry in pan.

Mix apples, sugar, cinnamon, and allspice; spread over cereal. Roll remaining pastry into rectangle; fold into thirds and gently place over apples; unfold. Beat reserved egg white until soft peaks form; spread over pastry.

Bake until crust is golden brown, 55–60 minutes. Mix powdered sugar, water, and vanilla until smooth and creamy; spread over warm crust. Sprinkle with nuts. Cut into bars, about 3x1½ inches.

Makes 30 bars.

Backpacker Bars

Keep your graham and peanut snack bars tucked securely away and out of sight. You will be the envy of every squirrel you encounter on the trail.

Preheat oven to 350 degrees.

In a large bowl, mix brown sugar, sugar, butter, vanilla, and eggs. Stir in flour, cereal, ¾ cup oats, baking powder, baking soda, and salt. Then stir in ¾ cup peanuts and ⅔ cup chocolate chips.

Spread in ungreased 13x9-inch pan.

Sprinkle with remaining ¼ cup peanuts, remaining ⅓ cup chocolate chips, and 2 tablespoons oats.

Bake 25–30 minutes or until golden brown. Cool completely (about 1 hour).

Makes 24 bars.

¾ cup brown sugar, packed

¾ cup sugar

¾ cup butter or margarine, softened

1 tsp. vanilla

2 eggs

1½ cups flour

1½ cups Golden Grahams cereal, crushed

¾ cup oats

½ tsp. baking powder

1 tsp. baking soda

½ tsp. salt

1 cup peanuts (chopped), with ¼ cup divided

1 cup chocolate chips, with ⅓ cup divided

2 Tbsp. oats

Banana Cereal Bars

A sweet, moist, banana-flavored bar with a touch of honey and cinnamon!

1½ cups Post Grape-Nuts cereal

¾ cup flour

¼ cup brown sugar, packed

½ cup butter

2 medium-size bananas, mashed

½ cup nonfat dry milk

¼ cup honey

1 egg

1 tsp. cinnamon

Preheat oven to 325 degrees. Grease a 13x9-inch baking pan.

In a large bowl, combine all ingredients. Pour mixture into prepared baking pan.

Bake for 30–35 minutes.

Breakfast in a Cookie Jar

Breakfast-in-a-Snap Cereal Bars

Now we know where the "snap" comes from in the Rice Krispies "snap, crackle, and pop."

Grease a 13x9-inch pan.

In a medium saucepan combine butter, sugar, milk, and salt. Cook to a soft-ball stage (approximately 240 degrees). Stir occasionally.

Remove from heat. Add vanilla and lemon juice.

In prepared pan, combine cereal, oats, and nuts. Pour hot syrup over cereal mixture. Stir lightly to coat cereal and nuts.

Spread mixture evenly. Sprinkle coconut on top. Press firmly into pan. Let set 3–4 hours. When firm, cut into squares.

¾ cup butter

1¼ cups sugar

1 cup oats

2 Tbsp. lemon juice

2 Tbsp. milk

½ tsp. vanilla

1 cup walnuts, chopped

1 cup flaked coconut

6 cups crispy rice cereal

Cereal Cookies

With just the right touch of sweetness, these wheat flake cookies have an orange twist you and your family will love!

½ cup butter

¼ cup sugar

1 egg

2 Tbsp. orange juice concentrate

1 Tbsp. orange peel, grated

1¼ cup flour

1 tsp. baking powder

½ cup wheat cereal flakes

Preheat oven to 350 degrees.

In a medium bowl, beat together butter, sugar, egg, orange juice, and orange peel until light and fluffy. Add flour and baking powder, beating until blended. Stir in cereal.

Drop by teaspoonfuls onto ungreased cookie sheet.

Bake 10–12 minutes or until edges are golden. Remove from cookie sheet to cool.

Makes 2 dozen cookies.

Cereal Yogurt Bars

A one-handed, satisfying snack bar with the portability of a cookie that is easy to eat anywhere, anytime!

Preheat oven to 350 degrees.

Combine 1½ cups of the cereal, ¾ cup flour, brown sugar, and cinnamon. Cut in butter until mixture is crumbly. Pat half of the mix into greased 8x8-inch pan.

Combine yogurt, egg, and 2 tablespoons flour. Spread over crumb mixture in pan; add remaining ½ cup cereal to the crumb mixture and sprinkle over yogurt mixture.

Bake for 30 minutes. Cool in pan. Cut into bars.

2 cups fruit and fiber cereal, reserving ½ cup

¾ cup flour

¼ cup brown sugar

½ tsp. cinnamon

½ cup butter

1 (8-oz.) cup flavored yogurt

1 egg, slightly beaten

2 Tbsp. flour

Grab-N-Go Cereal Bars

The name says it all. No time for a sit-down breakfast? Just grab one and go!
Deliciously convenient to carry and eat on the run!

¾ cup butter

1¼ cups sugar

2 Tbsp. milk

½ tsp. salt

2 Tbsp. lemon juice

1 Tbsp. vanilla

6 cups crispy rice
cereal

1 cup oats

1 cup walnuts,
chopped

¾ cup coconut, flaked

Combine butter, sugar, milk, and salt. Cook to a soft-ball stage (approximately 240 degrees) about 15 minutes. Stir occasionally. Remove from heat. Add lemon juice and vanilla.

In a greased 13x9-inch pan, combine cereal, oats, and nuts. Pour on hot syrup; stir lightly to coat cereal and nuts. Spread mixture evenly. Sprinkle coconut on top.

Press firmly into pan. Let set 4 hours. When firm, cut into squares.

Makes 30 bars.

Breakfast in a Cookie Jar

Mixed-up Cereal Cookies

Mixed with a little cookie dough, cereal takes on a new life.
Use several types of cereal when there is only a little left in the bottom of each bag!

Preheat oven to 350 degrees.

In a large bowl, cream together sugar and margarine. Beat in egg, orange juice, and vanilla.

Combine flour and baking powder. Mix dry ingredients into the first mixture until well blended. Stir in cereal.

Drop onto ungreased cookie sheet and bake for about 11 minutes.

Top baked cookie with a dollop of strawberry jam.

Makes 2 dozen.

Tip If using plain cereal such as corn or bran flakes, you might want to add chopped almonds, walnuts, or raisins.

½ cup sugar

½ cup margarine

1 egg

3 Tbsp. orange juice

1 tsp. vanilla

1¼ cups flour

1 tsp. baking powder

1½–2 cups of cereal, any variety

Peanut Butter Trail Bars

These bars are fiber-packed, portable, and soooo delicious!
Make a batch in the p.m. and you'll have a super-quick breakfast for the next a.m.

1 cup light corn syrup

½ cup brown sugar, packed

½ tsp. salt

1½ cups chunky peanut butter

1½ tsp. vanilla

1 cup nonfat dry milk

1 cup granola cereal

1 cup whole bran cereal

1 cup raisins

½ cup chocolate chips

Line a 13x9-inch pan with waxed paper.

In a heavy saucepan, stirring constantly, combine syrup, sugar, and salt; bring to a boil. Remove from heat; stir in peanut butter and vanilla.

Stir in dry milk, granola, bran cereal, and raisins. Let cool slightly. Add chocolate chips. Press into prepared pan.

Refrigerate 30 minutes. Cut into bars. Store in refrigerator.

Makes about 3 dozen.

Raisin-Filled Cereal Bars

If raisins are on your favorites list, add these cereal bars to your lunch or eat them as an after-school snack.

Raisin Filling: In a medium saucepan, combine sugar and cornstarch. Stir in raisins and water. Cook and stir over medium heat until thick and bubbly. Remove from heat; stir in lemon juice.

Prepare Raisin Filling as directed above and let cool. Preheat oven to 350 degrees.

Grease and flour a 13x9-inch baking pan.

Cream butter and brown sugar.

In a separate bowl, stir together flour, baking soda, and granola. Add dry ingredients to creamed mixture and mix well. Mixture will be crumbly.

Pat half of the mixture into prepared pan. Spread with raisin filling. Add an additional tablespoon of water to remaining crumb mixture; sprinkle on top of filling. Lightly press with hand.

Bake at 350 degrees for 30–35 minutes.

Cut into bars while still warm.

Makes 32 bars.

¾ cup butter, softened

½ cup brown sugar, packed

2 cups flour

½ tsp. baking soda

1½ cups granola cereal

Raisin Filling:

½ cup sugar

1 Tbsp. cornstarch

2 cups raisins

1 cup water

2 Tbsp. lemon juice

Ranger Cookies

Got scouts? These cookies are perfect for any length of hike.
Take them to the mountains or the lake for fuel to go all day.
P.S.—Do not feed the bears!

1 pouch or box (1 lb 1.5 oz.) oatmeal cookie mix

1 egg

1 Tbsp. water

1 tsp. vanilla

½ cup margarine or butter, softened

¾ cup crispy rice cereal

½ cup flaked coconut

½ cup peanut butter chips

½ cup chocolate chips

Preheat oven to 375 degrees.

In a large bowl, stir all ingredients until soft dough forms. Drop dough by rounded tablespoons onto ungreased cookie sheet 2 inches apart.

Bake 10–12 minutes or until edges are golden brown. Cool 1 minute; remove from cookie sheet.

Cool completely on a wire rack.

Store in an air-tight container.

Super Duper Snack Bars

If you want these bars baked fresh for breakfast, measure out the ingredients the night before. It only takes a few minutes to mix the batter and pop it in the oven.

Preheat oven to 350 degrees.

In a large bowl, mix brown sugar, sugar, butter, vanilla, and eggs until well blended. Stir in flour, corn flakes, and ¾ cup of the pecans, ⅓ cup candies, oats, baking soda, baking powder, and salt.

Spread in ungreased 13x9-inch pan. Sprinkle with remaining pecans and remaining ⅔ cup candies.

Bake until golden brown, 35–40 minutes; let cool. Cut into bars.

Makes 24 bars.

¾ cup brown sugar, packed

¾ cup sugar

¾ cup butter or margarine

1 tsp. vanilla

2 eggs

2 cups flour

1 cup corn flakes cereal, slightly crushed

1 cup pecans (chopped), with ¾ cup divided

1 cup candy-coated chocolate pieces, reserving ⅓ cup

¾ cup oats

1 tsp. baking soda

½ tsp. baking powder

½ tsp. salt

grains

A.M. Special Breakfast Cookies

½ cup vegetable oil

½ cup applesauce

½ cup brown sugar

1 egg

1 Tbsp. vanilla

2 Tbsp. lemon juice

½ cup oat bran

½ cup 7-grain cereal

½ cup flour

½ cup whole wheat flour

1 tsp. baking soda

½ tsp. salt

1 tsp. cinnamon

1 tsp. allspice

½ tsp. cloves

3 cups oats

1 cup raisins

¼ cup walnuts, chopped

Preheat oven to 350 degrees.

In a large mixing bowl, beat together oil, applesauce, and brown sugar. Add egg, vanilla, and lemon juice. Beat again.

In a separate bowl, sift together oat bran, 7-grain cereal, flours, baking soda, salt, and spices. Mix these ingredients with the wet mixture. Stir in oats. Fold in raisins and walnuts.

Place dough on ungreased cookie sheets by the spoonful. Bake 15 minutes or until golden. Remove from cookie sheet for cooling.

Breakfast Oatmeal Cookies

*These oat cookies are great for breakfast on the run
or a healthy pre-school snack!*

Preheat oven to 350 degrees.

In a large bowl, mix all ingredients in order. Use a tablespoon to make large scoops of dough. Flatten to ¾ inch.

Bake for 8–10 minutes on ungreased cookie sheet. Do not over bake. Remove from cookie sheet for cooling.

Makes 2 dozen cookies.

¾ cup brown sugar

½ cup margarine

1 egg

2 tsp. vanilla

3 medium-size ripe bananas, mashed

1 cup flour

⅔ cup whole wheat flour

2 tsp. pumpkin pie spice

½ tsp. baking soda

½ tsp. salt

2 cups oats, uncooked

Chewy Choco-Chip Granola Bars

These granola bars pack well for mid-day snacks or hiking trips.
These bars are a delicious and hearty alternative to doughnuts or pastries.

⅔ cup peanut butter

5 Tbsp. corn syrup

½ cup applesauce

½ cup brown sugar, packed

2 tsp. vanilla

3 cups rolled oats

1 cup chocolate chips

½ cup miniature marshmallows

½ cup toasted oat cereal

⅔ cup wheat germ

Preheat oven to 350 degrees. Grease a 13x9-inch baking pan.

In a large bowl, stir together the peanut butter, corn syrup, applesauce, brown sugar, and vanilla.

In a medium bowl, stir together oats, chocolate chips, mini marshmallows, cereal, and wheat germ.

Combine the peanut butter mixture and dry ingredients until evenly mixed. Press lightly into the prepared pan.

Bake for 25 to 30 minutes until slightly golden brown. Put the pan on a wire rack to cool. Cut into bars.

Makes 18 bars.

Playgroup Granola Bars

This batch is large enough to share with all your friends who run and swing!
Easy to mix and quick to bake.

Preheat oven to 350 degrees. Grease two 13x9-inch baking pans.

In a large bowl, mix together oats, flour, brown sugar, wheat germ, cinnamon, raisins, and salt. Make a well in the center, and pour in the honey, oil, eggs and vanilla. Mix well using your hands. Pat mixture evenly into the prepared pan.

Bake for 30–35 minutes in the preheated oven, until the bars begin to turn golden brown at the edges. Cool for 5 minutes, then cut into bars while still warm. Do not allow the bars to cool completely before cutting or they will be too hard to cut.

Makes 48 bars.

4 cups oats

2 cups flour

1½ cups brown sugar, packed

1 cup wheat germ

1½ tsp. cinnamon

1½ cups raisins

1½ tsp. salt

1 cup honey

1 cup vegetable oil

2 eggs, beaten

1 Tbsp. vanilla

Trail Blazin' Granola Bars

*These nutritious nut and honey-oat bars will keep you
stepping high and straight on the trail all day!*

2 cups oats

1 cup flour

¾ cup brown sugar

½ cup wheat germ

¾ cup raisins

1 tsp. cinnamon

½ tsp. salt

½ cup walnuts,
  chopped

½ cup oil

½ cup honey

1 egg

2 tsp. vanilla

Preheat oven to 350 degrees.

Line a 13x9-inch baking pan with aluminum foil and spray with vegetable oil.

In a large bowl, stir together oars, flour, brown sugar, wheat germ, raisins, cinnamon, salt, and walnuts.

In a small bowl, thoroughly blend oil, honey, egg, and vanilla. Pour into the flour mixture and mix by hand until the liquid is evenly distributed. Press evenly into the prepared baking pan.

Bake for 25–30 minutes, or until the edges are golden. Cool completely in pan. When pan is cool, turn out onto a cutting board and cut into bars.

Makes 20 bars.

no-bake

Frozen Snack Bars

*A refreshing, healthy snack alternative, perfect for a warm
summer afternoon. With this tasty make-ahead recipe, you can have a snack
that you'll look forward to enjoying!*

2 (8-oz.) cups fruit
flavored yogurt

2 cups fruit (chopped,
fresh, canned, or
frozen)

⅔ cup instant nonfat
dry milk

2 Tbsp. honey

2 cups Post Grape-
Nuts cereal

Place yogurt, fruit, dry milk, and honey in blender or food processor.

Blend until smooth, leaving fruit a little chunky.

Fold in 1½ cups cereal and pour into 8-inch square pan. Sprinkle with remaining cereal and gently press down for crunchy topping.

Put in freezer overnight.

Cut into 8 bars.

Wrap each in foil and leave in freezer.

Golden Flax Bars

I'll bet you never knew that adding alpha-linolenic acid (flax seed)
to your diet could taste so good!

Coat a 13x9-inch baking pan with nonstick cooking spray.

In a microwave-safe bowl, mix together the peanut butter, corn syrup, and brown sugar. Microwave for about 3 minutes on high. Stir in the ground flaxseed and vanilla, then pour the mixture over the crispy rice cereal and mix well.

Spread the mixture into the prepared pan and press down to form a dense sheet. Let the mixture sit for about 5–10 minutes until firmly set, then cut into bars.

Makes about 28 bars.

½ cup wheat cereal flakes

1 cup creamy peanut butter

1 cup corn syrup

1 cup brown sugar, packed

1 cup ground flaxseed

1 tsp. vanilla

5 cups crispy rice cereal

Microwave Granola Bars

This is a great get-the-kids-to-eat-something-they-think-is-dessert-but-is-really-healthy breakfast item!

1 cup brown sugar, packed

¼ cup sugar

½ cup butter

2 Tbsp. honey

½ tsp. vanilla

1 egg

1 cup flour

1 tsp. cinnamon

½ tsp. baking powder

¼ tsp. salt

1½ cups oats

1¼ cups crispy rice cereal

1 cup almonds, chopped

½ cup raisins

½ cup chocolate chips

½ cup wheat germ

Grease a 13x9-inch microwaveable dish.

In a large bowl, cream both sugars and butter until fluffy. Add honey, vanilla, and egg. Mix well.

Gradually blend in flour, cinnamon, baking powder, and salt at low speed. Stir in remaining ingredients.

Press firmly into bottom of dish. Microwave on medium for 8 minutes until set, rotating dish half a turn every 3 minutes during cooking.

Bars will firm as they stand and cool.

Makes 24 bars.

No-Bake Cereal Bars

Very colorful! A great recipe for kids.
Sure to be a hit at any potluck or family get-together!

Grease a 10x15-inch jelly roll pan.

In a large bowl, mix together the toasted oat cereal, rice cereal, peanuts, shredded coconut, and chocolate pieces; set aside.

In a medium saucepan over medium heat, stir together the corn syrup and sugar. Bring the mixture to a boil and cook until sugar is completely dissolved. Remove from heat. Quickly stir the peanut butter and vanilla into the sugar mixture.

Pour the mixture into the bowl with the cereal and mix well. Press into the prepared pan. Let stand until set.

Cut into 24 bars and serve.

4 cups toasted oat cereal

2 cups crispy rice cereal

2 cups dry roasted peanuts

¼ cup shredded coconut

2 cups candy-coated milk chocolate pieces

1 cup light corn syrup

1 cup sugar

1½ cups creamy peanut butter

1 tsp. vanilla extract

No-Bake Toasted Oat Bars

Try experimenting with different types of cereals.
Crispy rice cereal, graham cereal, and puffed wheat are all great!

1 cup sugar

1 cup corn syrup

1 cup peanut butter

6 cups toasted oat cereal

In a medium-size saucepan, combine sugar and syrup and bring to a boil. Add peanut butter immediately and stir well.

Remove from heat. Stir in cereal. Mix well until all the cereal is coated.

Pat into a 13x9-inch pan and let cool.

Keep in an airtight container, do not refrigerate.

Garnish, if desired, with a caramel sauce or melted milk chocolate chips.

Peanut Butter Cereal Bars

Creating a delicious treat does not always have to involve an oven.
This quick and easy-to-make snack bar can be a fun activity for the kids to make and eat!

Combine corn syrup, brown sugar, and salt, stirring constantly. Bring to a full boil. Stir in peanut butter.

Remove from heat. Stir in vanilla, corn flakes, rice cereal, and chocolate pieces.

Press into 9x9x2-inch pan. Chill 1 hour. Cut into bars.

Makes 12 bars.

½ cup light corn syrup

¼ cup brown sugar

dash salt

1 cup peanut butter

1½ tsp. vanilla

1 cup corn flakes

2 cups rice cereal

1 cup semi-sweet
chocolate chips

Fruit and Honey No-Bake Breakfast Bars

These versatile bars are at home in lots of places.
Try one for a quick energy boost, a brown-bag treat, an after-school
snack, or anytime—they're just good!

1½ cups chunky peanut butter

1 cup honey

¾ cup brown sugar

5 cups bran or oat flake dry cereal

1 cup dried fruit pieces, bite size

Combine peanut butter, honey, and brown sugar in large saucepan. Bring to a boil, stirring constantly. Remove from heat. Quickly stir in cereal and fruit bits.

Mix well.

Using buttered spatula or waxed paper, press mixture evenly into a greased 13x9-inch pan.

Cool 10 minutes before cutting.

Makes 18 bars.

Peanut and Cocoa-Cereal Bars

Double this recipe to guarantee there will be plenty.
These are always a real hit with teenagers!

Blend together peanut butter, butter, and powdered sugar. With hands, mix in cereal, crushing it slightly.

Line an 8x8-inch baking pan with aluminum foil. Press cereal mixture into pan. Sprinkle with peanuts and press in firmly. Chill for several hours.

To serve, pull up foil to remove cooled cookie from pan. Cut into bars.

Makes 16 bars.

1 cup chunky peanut butter

2 Tbsp. butter

1¼ cups powdered sugar, sifted

3 cups chocolate-flavored corn puffs

1 cup peanuts, coarsely chopped

index

C

F

G

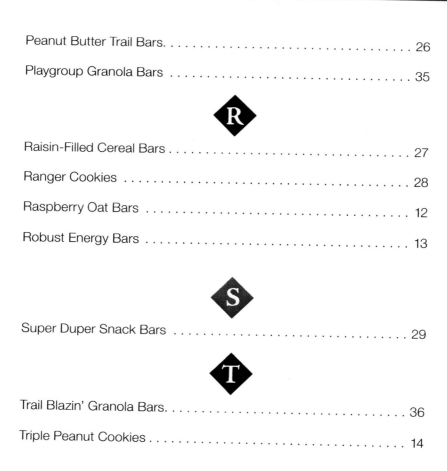

About the Author

Carlene Duda attended Ricks College (now BYU—Idaho) and Brigham Young University. She is a culinary writer, teacher, and cook.

Her award-winning recipes have been published in newspapers and copyrighted by C&H Sugar Company.

Carlene lives in Puyallup, Washington, with her husband, Scott, and their four children.